Time of Sky

Castles in the Air

— A dream journal

Time of Sky

Castles in the Air

— A dream journal

Ayane Kawata

Translated by Sawako Nakayasu

Litmus Press

ISBN: 978-1-933959-08-5
Library of Congress Control Number: 2010921170

Cover art: "Trees and Glass," 2004, by Mauro Zamora
acrylic latex and watercolor on canvas, 12 x 16 inches

Design & typesetting by HR Hegnauer | hrhegnauer.com
Interior text typeset in Eurostile and Meridien.

Litmus Press is a program of Ether Sea Projects, Inc., a 501(c)(3) non-profit literature and arts organization. Dedicated to supporting innovative, cross-genre writing, the press publishes the work of translators, poets, and other writers, and organizes public events in their support. We encourage interaction between poets and visual artists by featuring contemporary artworks on the covers of our full-length books and in the pages of *Aufgabe*, our annual literary journal. By actualizing the potential lingustic, cultural, and political benefits of international literary exchange, we aim to ensure that our poetic communities remain open-minded and vital.

This book is made possible by public funds from the New York State Council on the Arts, a State agency. Additional support for our books comes from individual members and donors. All contributions are fully tax-deductible.

State of the Arts

NYSCA

Litmus Press
PO Box 25526
Brooklyn, New York 11202-5526
litmuspress.org

Distributed by Small Press Distribution
1341 Seventh Street
Berkeley, California 94710
spdbooks.org

Time of Sky

(1969)

1

Blood always blood
As blue is blue
Incessant explosion of a thirst-ripened orange

2

A kiss on the fountain that grows pigeon-like anywhere upon the
trembling mirror that exposes itself

3

The innocent window
Flung inwards
And further in
Screams are forced to run radiantly and full speed

4

Don't call
Don't bundle the yellow lilies that fly about
Don't eavesdrop on the egg

5

I discover a newly drowned body amidst the geometric scene
welling up in the sky of my eyes

6

The peninsula
The rail
The exploded branches
The breasts
The netting
The white plate—
Fly!

7

Because the blue sky is so swift
I must lap up the lukewarm blood seeping into the mirror

8

The Morpho butterfly
Who crosses over
Lighter than semen
Snatches what away
From an eye called an eye

9

A transparent clock is constructed while being kneaded by the
foul breath of things which sprout

1 0

A scream inside a fish
A table is a table
The raped orange becomes the blue sky

1 1

Tumbling recklessly while mincing the surroundings is a wound
or an ear or the yellow lily

1 2

The pigeon
Does not grow any lighter than that
Does not go dark
Draws yellow on the spine

1 3

The woman who drank the glass window will have a seizure at
dawn and tremble to her fingertips

1 4

Hey
Let's sound the organ and
Blow away the woods bulging with sparkling eggs

15

Please give me the fishy stars born by the coral trees with black
nostrils that inflate into the sun

16

The word
Of the right breast
Of the bag under the eye
Of the leg
Of the fire filling my fingertips
Of the wave sound of blood
In my eye

1 7

While ceaselessly painting the cranial sky blue
The blood must train inside the brass instrument

1 8

A slope that rises up
From anywhere
Stray dogs loiter about
And dawn imposes the birth of an unexpected bird

1 9

From the trace of the incontinent blood of an angel walking along
holding some sky cut out with a glass cutter, the dawn—

2 0

In the insanely quiet
Sky of the eyes
A blank sheet of paper rouses the suggestion of a peculiar flower
and blows up

21

The ridgeline of the woman who offers up her entire body to an invisible light becomes the first blue aria of spring

22

Shh
Did you see the sky open
Roses are islands of distraction
Targeted by a distant voice

2 3

Noon
I pass through both my ears barefoot and become an eyeless blue
sheet and undulate

2 4

The pebble shoots up blood
The fig tree sings
In the clouds of butter the newborn eyelids have trouble with
the glare

2 5

Is that the sky cleaving just as I've reached the top of the midsummer midday stairs filling my arms?

2 6

Incessantly—
Birds
A blast of wind
Flowing lips
Poplars desperately flaring up—
Come!

2 7

Will the lark's vein blow up
Or will an earful of the distant blue make its way inside

2 8

Lips thrust out
Dodging lilac sludge
Veering from the stairs
A bored angel turns the corner

2 9

The birds that walk impatiently around the row of ginkgo trees
sparkling in the fainted woman

3 0

At the speed of a reed of blood crawling about the brain
As if to assault—
Sing

3 1

Teeth of light irritably chew apart the wheat field and it becomes
a convulsive midday

3 2

Ears are covered up with the window breath of plaster
Stars decompose violently
There is no canoe
Buttercups bloom in profusion

3 3

Midday

Until the massacre in the embers of the eyes of the lark falling full
speed subside!

3 4

Have the wheels gone numb

Or are they fountains

Or are the lacerated branches sparkling

3 5

Until my sky is cornered into that organ that is faster than a blast
of wind, faster than a lily bud

3 6

The light the smell of blood
All the larks go mad and
The fountain grows thick and
The pot opens its mouth

3 7

O naked women letting out screams and passing through the invisible automatic doors of the blue sky

3 8

Breasts that hatch
Like music
Mirrors resound and melt
The sky goes missing

3 9

Traveling the endless noonday street in the eyes of myself traveling
the endless noonday street in my eyes

4 0

I admire the kind fingers which peel
The wilderness
The calendar
The eggshell

4 1

Go to sleep—
The stairs beginning anywhere connect to the noon sky without
a single egg

4 2

O whip
Beating its wings toward the invisible sky
While dragging out that final-hour scream

4 3

The numerous street corners are nothing but bright and pollen keeps raining down upon the deserted hamlet

4 4

Collect the evening primrose nectar and bundle up the youthful arms and pinch off the cloud larvae and—
To the breakfast table

4 5

The noon sky

Does not depart

Inside the cup an enormous tongue goes numb and perishes

4 6

Slipping away into the garden that ants dream of, until an
enchanting blue triangle is sniffed out

4 7

Without a sound
Soft ears keep colliding frequently and
A south wind must be hatching

4 8

The saliva of the sky is at any time melting the poles and lark eggs
and instruments and shining

4 9

Thrusting up the bare sole of a foot
Making the grape seed shine
What wakes the sudden artery?

5 0

How long will the women be gasping as they open and close their
arms in the towering forest of mirrors

5 1

The table
The lark going corrupt
The shore
The fingers
The shards of mirror
Burn up

5 2

O dog!
You best wander unsteadily through the bright lukewarm fields
of brains

5 3

From the eucalyptus tree
To the nails
To the ant nest
Rippling
There is a village that is unable to stop quivering

5 4

The fingers that have finished arranging my blood on graph paper
will see their first break of dawn

5 5

O crocodile

Noon in the summer of a flash

Let's starve to death gently without even a scream

5 6

The stray dogs that swarm around sniffing blood in the corn field
that rustles like luminous lies!

5 7

Fur swimming in the sky
Carrots
A horde of innocent lips
Where did they come from

5 8

Midday when salt pours down upon the sea of blood
O canoe that glides along awakening the stars

5 9

As if in a dream
Ferociously
I see larks in a sky without larks

6 0

What are the midday angels evading as they vomit aluminum
feathers

6 1

Inside the egg
Music as transparent as flesh
That makes an assault on tomorrow
To the clouds
To the fish
Until it becomes seed

6 2

Everything leaps
Into the blue sky as bright as the blood in the hand mirror that
cannot be seen for all eternity

6 3

Is it the light
Or the roses
Is the shore being torn apart
Or are the maggots awakening

6 4

Now isn't there an ear that tries to turn itself over by any means
by scratching apart its inner walls like a flower

65

Where have the birds gone to lurk
It is not time
Inside my pulse I am making empty crystals

66

The sky awakens to a seemingly momentary daybreak and
continues feeding drips of blood into a distant ear

6 7

Did you see
The flute cutting the grass
And cutting the mirror
And the internal organs
And setting fire to it over beyond

6 8

The sky does not shout
In the blank sheet of paper the sheep do not even make the sound
of their eyelids opening

6 9

Is it a blizzard
Or will the diamonds soften
Or is it the woods with lukewarm breath continuing to crumble
while continuing to grow

7 0

O insects hunting in the air with their necks bowed down by the
summer light!

7 1

When the one single window
Opens
There is no sound
Deep in the snowstorm
A cup that does not sleep a wink
Breathes

7 2

The shards of glass
The pigeon
The sharpening nipple
And the onion fields are rubbed and smashed and a beastly aria—

7 3

In the sky in the hole drilled into my heart I see a forest burning
up like eternity!

7 4

Is it the blood
Or the mirage
Or the radiantly crazed school of sea bream
That flutters

7 5

O mirror that shudders fearfully in a moment of daybreak and
fertilizes a copious number of lips

7 6

To drink
The water of the sky
The bud of fire that lurks in the sludge of the brains of the cow
A whirlwind from
The egg

7 7

There the fossilized eyes and wings and fingers choke their throats
and murmur to each other and—
Spring

7 8

This is not an orientation
While drowning to death vast numbers of larks
The blood has a dream

7 9

The tiny smashed comfort of the meat that is chopped and blown
away by the midday flute—

8 0

How far will
The pigeons of light
Flapping their wings
While rotting away
Spread
The table of summer

8 1

Shoot
The women covering up their kneecaps and squatting in an enormous blank sheet of paper

8 2

The two hands that shouted are falling!
Vomit blood—
They're violets
Fall over laughing—

83

What kindly fingers are setting fire to the apricots flowering in
the sky that brims over with ultraviolet rays

84

Peeling off another slice
Of the fingers of mica
I watch the fluttering of the locked up bay

85

Let the throat and uterus and little branches of bones belonging to
the girl seduced by the lark and hung upside down all burn up

86

A sudden gust
A school of anchovies
Fire leaking from the nose of the cow
A bouquet of
Glass spheres—

8 7

From my naked body to the blank paper
To the sprinting giraffe to the egg to someone I do not yet see
The sky going crazy

8 8

It is a brain that grows entranced and numb from smelling lilacs
at their peak in the raised axe

8 9

Those that awaken from touching the flight
Of the eggs that dream
Mark the passing of time
In complete confusion
And the sky is wet like fish

9 0

The diamonds tear the sky apart and convulse the blood by daybreak to the very last drop

Castles in the Air

— A dream journal

(1991)

Horse

For some reason I acquire a horse, but I don't know how to harness it. A rope around its neck would probably be painful. I try to remember how I had seen a horse bridled, but I don't quite know how to make it bite. I wonder if it will eat grass when it gets hungry. Or if it will be okay if I tie it under a tree and it rains and gets wet. I can't find a stable anywhere. Then the horse disappears and becomes my younger sister. She lies down upon the bare night grass and tries to sleep. I think she'd get cold like that, but she rolls around as if to say, "I'm fine."

Grown thin

I go to visit Y in what is perhaps her study or dressing room, where the walls are plastered over with pictures, and letters with drawings, and there are little doll-like things hanging. It is like the room of a young girl. Y has grown thin and is bald, and the adolescent Y is seated sideways in front of the mirror stand with eyes vacantly open. Her legs are all bone. There is a bandage on her bared bottom as well as bruises. It's a painful sight. Y does not at all notice my presence nearby as she sits in a daze surrounded by windowless walls. Coming to understand that this may be the end of our relationship, I look at the pictures on the wall and read some of the letters.

Translator's Note:
The initials representing people's names are unchanged from the original text with the exception of "Y," which has replaced "I" so as to avoid confusion with the personal pronoun.

Lino's vacation home

Lino lives in a vacation home, and Y is there too. Approaching us from behind, Y shows us two wooden toys that look like pigeons with wheels. Y says he made it for Lino and I, but I look at it thinking it doesn't look very interesting at all.

Lino gets up first and shows us around the yard. It is cool and damp and there is a thick growth of dark trees. At the bottom of the stone steps is a cage. Inside are fourteen or so yapping little dogs, and a topless Indio boy. The boy seems to be in charge of keeping the dogs. Lino and Y talk to the boy from outside the cage as if it were perfectly natural. We feel like we cannot ask any questions. Y bites Lino's shoulder through his shirt. The boy can make pistols and is good at performing tricks with them, and it seems that Lino has brought him here from an Osaka circus.

Later we are led through a long, narrow, monastery-like hallway towards some dark place.

Stripes

In the room of an apartment I try to make love with someone I met on the airplane. The body of this young man is completely covered in oily stripes. He is sticky and I fear it might rub off on me.

Overpass at night

I arrive alone at the station in the middle of the night. The platform is elevated, and I go down the stairs of the overpass, but it is so dangerous I need to hold the handrails on both sides. For the time being I let the things in my hand fall down to the ground. When I make my way to the bottom, with both hands on the handrails, my young mother is waiting for me in the darkness below, wearing a shawl. "Where are your things?" she asks slightly reproachfully. When I tell her, "I dropped them from up above," she regretfully says, "Oh." "Look, it's no problem," I say casually as I quickly retrieve from the dark ground all the things I had dropped from above, picking up my short pencils, notebook, paperback, and empty lunchbox. "This is enough." I think that it is a well-organized pile of belongings, if I do say so myself.

D

D's heart has already grown apart from mine. We have promised to go our separate ways in the morning, but for now we are staying in some small-town hotel. Early in the morning D's friend comes to the room and says, "Once you leave her, it will eliminate your expenses," as if trying to get him to buy a motorcycle. And then it appears the two will depart for a trip.

I pay my share of the room to the hotel clerk and go out. The town has many stone steps everywhere. I don't have any idea where to go. There is a light on in a building with its door open, where they are either selling or simply exhibiting something. I walk by it feeling very meek.

Falling apart

Repeatedly, something falls apart. I simply have the actual feeling
that I accept that "this is how things fall apart," but there is nothing
I can see. Its concrete texture has flowed past and disappeared.

Backside of the pool

I go around to the backside of the pool I frequent only to find it completely vacant. I think that if they would only turn its walls into a tank and add some fish, it would liven up the space. On one hand I could dive into the ocean and catch some fish, or I could spread some transparent instant products loose in the water, which would immediately turn into live fish and begin swimming. In either case they'd be fish from southern waters, with three heads or nothing but heads or some such peculiar tropical fish. I like the thought of throwing them in with no consideration for variety, but there are concerns such as feeding, so I need to make friends with someone who knows a lot about nature.

The following day when I visit, the space has completely changed. There are several tanks for young fish, the bookshelves are teeming with books, and there are even specimens arranged in a row. It's turned into a stuffy museum. The man in charge of the pool proudly says, "It's so much better now," and "Because we filled such a large tank with water all of a sudden, the whole district had a power outage last night," using a model of the district to explain. I listen vacantly, not caring anymore.

Ability to take action

A man places his hand on my tense, frozen back and inspects it, concluding, "On a scale of large, medium and small, your ability to take action is small."

Gently

There are several people in the room, and the elderly person glaring into space with both hands on the wall seems to be a poet. We pair up and gently start to dance. "Can you dance?" I ask, though these are my first steps as well. His face overlaps with that of my deceased father.

White lettering

A boy of about five years of age is showing me something like a clear sheet of plastic. Something is written in white lettering on the front and back in several languages, but because it is transparent the letters overlap with each other and I am unable to read it. There is no need to read this, there's no difference whether I read it or not, I think.

Cup of blood

I hold a cup, trying to drink the blood coursing through it, but I just can't bring myself to drink it.

Organ

It looks like there is an athletic field enclosed within a tall iron fence in a very lonely place by the river. There is a row of wooden bungalows that serve as convalescent home buildings. I find relief in returning, though I believe there is danger in this type of complete surrendering of the self.

The patients have gathered in the auditorium and my younger sister is playing the organ. A duplicate of my sister is singing by her side at the same time, or they are singing a duet. No one else sings. As I listen, I am moved—then she seems to happily notice my presence—*big sister.*

Apparently the patients are never allowed out again. A desolate feeling of resignation can be felt on this barren athletic ground without a single tree. There are some patients jostling against each other by the iron fence—it seems they are forming a line and waiting their turn, but two or three of them have caused a ruckus and there is now a commotion. Perhaps this is not a convalescent home for tuberculosis patients after all, but an insane asylum.

On the grass

Suddenly a farmer-like man grabs me into an embrace on the grass and with a very serious expression kisses my ankles with his nose. "With your mouth," I say, but he replies solemnly, "It must be with my nose." He is the offender after all, so I give up and leave it up to him, until something like rapture wells up in me and I shiver, at which point the man nods as if to say "Yes" in confirmation. He reminds me of someone, maybe the milkman.

Travel scene

I go on a trip, and take in the sight of a deceased person's bedding being slid piece by piece down the corridor of a tall tree and shoved down below, which leaves a lingering resonance in my ears. Later, there is nowhere for me to spend the night.

Mario Marinetti

A dim studio. I bring my face close to that of Mario Marinetti as I make wave patterns in a box of sand with my hands. These undulations reach Mario Marinetti—I am thinking that this, too, is a way of touching—and I see that he, too, is happily peering into the box.

Caresses

My younger sister and I are caressing each other. We stimulate each other, touching each other's nipples, going into a craze. It seems to be a hospital room. There are only two of us left and there is nothing left for us to do but to love one another. Seeing my sister relaxed and smiling in spite of this whitish loneliness makes me feel slightly relieved.

The number two

a

In the darkness of space there are small substances scattered and placed in a circular pattern. I feel that K's head and the head of his wife exist side by side like the halves of a walnut. I also feel that the consciousness of my crime is flowing behind me, and there is also a sense of defeat.

b

It must be daybreak—I watch a lily bud growing full in the dim darkness. In the air, two life-sized lily buds breathe lightly and grow full.

With an infant

A man is chasing me—so in order to escape I try to have a relationship with an infant. The idea is to drive the man away by having him see me make love to the infant. The infant understands the situation completely.

University city

I leave my bags in a Tokyo hotel and go for a walk and end up in a university city. I realize that this is the university where J is a cultural anthropologist, so I try to visit J's office. I ask some students how to get there but I am thwarted by the complicated system of color-coded numbers and letters that organize the elevators and corridors and I am unable to figure it out. However, in this process I discover the phone number to the poet Y's office. "Hello," I say, but there is no answer even though the phone line has connected. Eventually Y comes out of the office with some students and I pile into a jeep along with them all, and we take off. The young women are completely naked with clear blisters all over, and Y goes around popping them with a needle. I suspect that those blisters are a result of fire injuries inflicted by Y. I guess that's what the class was all about.

Thorn, like a knife

There is a fork in the road, and to one side, a small tree shines on the dirt path. The twigs and leaves have been shorn off of a few branches, which are now naked and gleaming white. The tree looks like a thorn, like a knife. This is the path I must take.

Walk

I go back to my hometown and take a walk with my father. We walk vigorously along the riverfront and have a good time. My father says, "I usually can't walk this fast because your mom doesn't like it," and I think about how kind he is, as always.

The following day I am invited to my father's house for dinner. My mother is in her sickbed. It must have become too difficult to save her, as people have already gathered near. My father says to me gently, "This morning on the way down the stairs, I only touched her shoulder a little and she fell. Because I had been thinking I would like to go for more walks." This person who is my mother has grown fat; she seems like an insensitive type of woman I don't recognize. I feel calm knowing that no one will realize how I am feeling towards my father. And from now on my father and I will be able to take all the walks we want.

Rosé

In a shared hospital room there is a large man in the bed next to me with a weight on his chest, leg suspended, wearing heavy shoes. He has been hospitalized in order to lose weight. He reaches in from the side of my bed and touches my body, but I wordlessly move out of the way.

When he is about to leave the hospital, I go along too. It seems that he is the night watchman for the storehouse and he fiddles with the switch in a small room, but there is no telling what this man will do.

I also learn that this monster of a man is actually the leader of a gang. When I buy groceries at a store run by this man, I say that I don't need alcohol because I don't drink, but he insists I buy this bottle of rosé. It seems like the lettering on the label that says *rosé* and the light peach-colored liquid are swaying, as if ordering me to "be amorous." I am ashamed of myself for having made such an expensive purchase. I have a strange feeling that I might eventually allow for that first relationship with this monster of a man, proffering my body out for the man to touch.

Concert

I promise two boys who might be brothers that I would go to the concert with them and the adults harshly reproach me for this. Mr. Suzuki is playing at the concert hall but I fall deep into conversation with the boys and have no idea what instrument he played and how he played it. The audience applauds, Mr. Suzuki bows on the stage, but I have a dubious feeling as to why he is even taking a bow. Later I see Mr. Suzuki and am unable to admit that I hadn't listened to a thing, but I suspect he already knows this.

Castles in the Air

N o

I am seated at a restaurant patio on an island, across the table from a young film director. An Italian asks, "How was the island?" and the director says, "There were many things I did not like," brushing off the place quite brusquely. "Of the Italian cities, if you go to Ferrara, the people are quite nice," I say, but the director says that he is headed for Zurich tomorrow on his way back to London. And then, still without expression, he mumbles, "Once is not enough for you," and I think he is talking about marriage. Then he asks, "Have you ever been in a mental institution?" and I say, "No."

The white cloud

Just as a white cloud swirled and gushed upward, the figure of a large swan appeared, as if in agony. And then the flock of birds crossing the sky one after another looks similar to clouds floating by. There is a single clear thread shining—it seems that they are moving towards an unpolluted continent, lead by this thread.

The garden at night

A hotel like a vacation home, with a garden. I must have been here a few times in the past, as the proprietress seems quite fond of me. She insinuates that I've brought a new man and I rather proudly reply, "I've known him for twenty-eight years." Things are different from before—my heart no longer feels restrained. I feel comforted deep in my heart, as if a long period has finally come to an end. In the garden at night he is standing still, the figure of a young man.

A d r a m a t i c a c t i o n

Someone has the main role, and we are all divided into groups and instructed to perform a dramatic action. Our group is in a village—some enter a barn or lie down in the street, or embrace a large dog. Eventually these actions catch the attention of the police. We knew from the start that we would have problems, I think, as each group member shows proof of identity to the police, speaking in French. I myself am invisible and it seems that no one can see me from the outside. I do not have to prove my identity. I feel that this is what it means to be a poet.

Eyelids peeled

A banker or a stage actor, a man I think I've known before, approaches me from down the corridor. I am thinking that his glowing smile means that he wants to touch me, when suddenly, standing there, the man peels back both my eyelids and inspects me. I grow cold to him after that and nothing happens.

Rock particle

I am walking and I pick up a white rock particle with many layers of striations. Here I can see the entire orientation of my life appear in the striations, and I am filled with a soundless, succinct feeling.

Skeletal people

On a dark stage, it appears that men are standing around exchanging deep kisses. There is only a single black platform for a set. The man who I think might be with me is sleeping on the platform away from everyone else with a cloth covering him. There is a profound sense of homosexuality. I'm not sure how I ended up in this place. When I go into the next room the air feels similar—there are several men, along with some skeletal people, speaking secretively. A young, slender skeletal person gently pats my head. This puts me at ease, and I too will sleep tonight on the black platform with something covering me.

Gladiolas

My father seems to have found another woman and is going to leave the house, so he is packing up. He is even taking things like pots. Feeling lonely, I pull my father's hairs out one strand at a time and they turn into gladiolas. I make a bouquet of it and thrust it out, leaning on my father and crying. My mother is quietly there, like a shadow, and her attitude is not very clear.

Three dreams

1

I realize that when it comes to the human shape and form, regardless of which direction people walk in, we all walk parallel to each other as if carrying magnetism. Like drops of rain.

2

When I visit that house, just inside the entry is someone in a steel basket, crouched like a bat. And there is a young man holding a deformed old person with smashed-in eyes and white waxy skin. He is petting those smashed-in eyes with his hands. Very good care is being taken of someone deformed like the devil.

3

The people who have gathered in this public bath all still have their clothes on. The bath is empty and there is no hot water. It's not that each person is in front of a faucet doing laundry, but there is a desolate feeling in the way they are all hunched over doing something.

Forehead

T.T.'s forehead shines slightly transparently and I can see that the skin is very finely textured. Knowing this, I feel somehow happy.

This kind of method

Under the assumption that I am covered with cloth and cannot
see, I follow some man. I understand that this is the only method.
The man seems to be a Spaniard.

Hedge

When M recognizes that I am standing in front of his house, he waves his hand as if to shoo me away—"Go away, quickly." It seems that he has just emerged from the studio and is carrying some materials. In the garden greenery, his slightly tired but beautiful wife is playing the piano placed by the hedge. Beyond that, two young sisters with matching eye-catching clothes are playing by the water. I retreat into the distance along the hedge.

Covered with spots

Trapped and walking around in a cold, gray building of reinforced concrete, there are groups of men and women, and of men only, who are mingling and appear to have no means of escape. Everyone is completely naked, and because of the disease are covered with spots and running around in confusion. I go down the stairs to find that there are numerous corpses abandoned on the concrete floor of the basement. There is no escape besides this.

Near the entrance I meet a young man who has just entered the building. I blurt out, "You might want to reconsider." He asks, "Do you want to run away?" "Yes," I say, desperately, but as we try to escape together we are discovered by a female guard. The young man casually lies to her, saying, "We just want to be alone for a little bit," and quickly pushes open a different door and we are able to step out into the dark yard.

After that we run like crazy. Without worrying about being naked, we run through the night air.

A white box

I am lying down inside a box surrounded by thin white walls when I sense that Y is approaching from above. I am unable to hide my desire for Y, but eventually I am able to tuck it away completely inside my heart.

A quiet person

I am sitting on a bench thinking about poetry, either at a bus stop or at a makeshift office. There is a quiet person who has been waiting for me without saying a word. A tall, introverted, somewhat lonely person. We hold each other and kiss. He grabs a large white swan that suddenly appears in the air. Then, the sight of him hunched over and pulling out swan feathers that have stabbed him in the arm seems tortured, like vomiting.

Eating with the dog

When I return home after a long absence I am told that the dog has lost its appetite and has not eaten in a long time. I go to take a look and find that it has been tied to a gas pipe and my mother has forgotten to plug the pipe with the stopper that is attached to the collar. This is why the dog has collapsed. Mother closes the pipe as if it were no big deal and the dog quickly gets back up. Right then I see a transparent figure, like the dog's soul, slip out and up.

The small tube that has folded up to palm-size becomes another dog. Its limbs are like that of a human baby and it has an adult-like face like that in a painting of the Sienese School. But the understanding is that this is a dog. This dog has not been eating at all. Its skin is white and it seems to lack energy, but what is strange to me is that it is a foldable dog that can survive without eating.

Tatami mats

A small room lined with tatami mats. The man is wearing glasses and sits cross-legged, watching me dance naked as if shining a light on me. Gradually I grow short of breath and my dancing turns into struggling while the man continues to watch intently.

An overflowing sensation

I am swimming in a pool—and this sensation that flows over me as I swim takes on a strange coloring, like seaweed or paper scraps. It breathes and floats up around my body.

Heavy bag

A school after hours, like a green botanical garden. There I am entangled with D and we make love upon the grass as a matter of course. Then, after D leaves I must carry a heavy bag and walk across the large, empty campus. There is barbed wire all around.

Tree-lined path

I am finally able to see him, having discovered the university where he worked. I am thrown off because he has changed so much—beyond recognition—but I do recognize him just from his voice. I tell him, "In my dreams, you were exactly like in the past," to which he replies, "So were you." We decide to walk around until the next class period begins. There are tree-lined paths, and it's been a while since we've walked along them.

I awaken, all worked up. It suddenly occurs to me how I should live from now on—I need to go find him. Our ties have been broken, however, and I wonder why, since then, I have had to live with my emotions repressed, and if it was because there were things about the world that I needed to learn.

Wrists like megaphones

A middle-aged burglar steps in through the double-paned glass doors of the wide patio. The burglar seeks to hold negotiations regarding the future. Although my mother is there too, it is my job to deal with him, so we draw up a contract in which I become the burglar's lover. Our intercourse is unsatisfactory, but he says, "Please make do with this," and it almost feels like he is taking care of me.

The man arrives for a second time, saying that he will come back to get me in ten minutes. I quietly go after him to see where he goes, following him into the depths of a dark church. There are confessional boxes all along the sides. Surprised to discover the man's religious devotion, I also go into a box and confess something. On the other side is the feeble voice of a nun with very little presence. Perhaps it is the wife of the man.

When I go out the man has already finished confession and is standing in the hallway. He is about to slide on his wrists, which look like megaphones made out of cardboard.

Pale blood

As I crush the fleas running all over the chest of a white puppy, it leaves behind dots of pale blood on its white fur.

Castles in the air

At the top of a narrow staircase with numerous convoluted turns is the room where I am sleeping with a man—it seems we have rented this room. I have to run an errand and go all the way down those stairs, but by the time I return the man is already sleeping with a different woman. Ah, castles in the air—

To Settignano

It is my younger sister's birthday so I suggest we go to Settignano for a walk. "It's nice there, let's go," I say, but she worries, "We would have to leave Mom alone." "It's a bit far for Mother to travel," I say, but then our mother says, "It's fine, I'm coming too. We'll get to Girone and come back to town on the #36 bus." Though we had never spoken of this, she is completely in the know as she points at the map to the road by the river Arno.

Instantaneously

It all seems like an instantaneous thing, that I am standing around chatting with A, who from there disappears down the elevator behind him.

For the exhibition

There are papers and materials organized on a steel rack; it could be M's storage space. I have been boarding in this place and feel rather unsettled. Though I thought I had locked the door before I went to bed, before I know it M and his assistants are standing near and watching over me dubiously. A weak electric current is run through me and my screams are recorded, all of which seems to be in preparation for the work to be shown in M's next exhibition.

The nail

I push a man down into a hole that is like an underground pipe. The torn and festering face of this dead man. Y's mother also squats down and peers into the pipe, and we wonder if it is really Y. Eventually I am held suspect for this. All the while the nail is pounded into the coffin I feel like I could scream, as if the nail were pounding into my shoulder.

Frog

For some reason an airmail package has arrived in my absence, containing a frog and a dirty dish. I have no use for the dirty dish so I throw it away. The small frog is brown and shiny, almost mineral-like. I wonder how to take care of it—and if it will be able to acclimate and survive on Italian soil if I set it free here. I make a miniature garden out of sand and water for it, but I worry that it isn't enough water and I wonder how it will survive the winter. I am at a loss.

Mitsuko's house. Her husband has returned from Switzerland, and while the couple is talking, the frog goes to the kitchen and eats dried sardines. The frog seems to be carnivorous but what should I feed it. And then it comes time to say goodbye to Mitsuko. Not without a feeling of relief, we hold each other's shoulders and say our goodbyes.

That Schillinger

A job advertising Schillinger. First I need to experience his work, then I am to sing a song in front of an audience in the auditorium. "Look this over," I am told as I am handed a small sheet of paper with the score printed on it. It's the kind of simple song I have no desire to sing.

I am hospitalized in order to experience this Schillinger. Nearby, children are messing up the bed and running around the floor— no one appears to be sick. I am supposed to be experiencing Schillinger, though no one has told me what kind of work that entails. Feeling uncertain, I ask a nurse, who simply explains, "You put Schillinger inside your genitals and spread it out. Afterwards, it's nice." I didn't know it was that kind of advertising. The photo in the newspaper of the farm-equipment-like apparatus—and the thought of having part of that thing enter my body gives me the chills. Even if it's nice afterwards I don't even have a partner right now, I think, and get out of bed in a hurry. "I quit," I say, and the nurse says, "Oh," nodding expressionlessly. Absolutely not—what do they mean, singing a song? My anger has yet to abate.

A frightening midget

A gypsy woman grabs my hand and bends my fingers back to look, saying, "You will change jobs." I don't know what that means, since there is nothing for me to do but write, when she says, "You will become a wife." And sure enough, as she predicted, it seems I am to become the partner of a frightening midget with his eyes bared, from I don't know what country. The fingers on his hands vary in length and have no fingernails, with black scars where the nails should be. W, O, and Y all come out in their usual appearance and I am talking to them in a good mood—loudly, even.

Girlfriend

I am spending the night at T's house. She is a good cook and the meat she has made is delicious. It seems that she has sliced the fresh meat directly off the cow herself. When it's time to go to bed she takes out a futon from the closet for me, but the old futon has been left folded and unused in the closet for so long that there are large ticks and paper wasps on it. She immediately brushes off the ticks, then tears off one of the paper wasp's wings before hitting it. Suddenly two sumo wrestlers enter. We are so scared that we are frozen sitting in front of the desk, hanging our heads and sniffling like children.

Stray cats and dogs

1

In the darkness of the movie theater the audience members gradually get up off their seats, partner up with whomever, and begin to dance.

2

A scene in which there are stray cats and dogs, and they are the only ones with a real presence.

3

My younger sister blows about the ashes in an ashtray and does other childish things, making me very nervous.

Baby

I have had a baby and am already feeding it baby food. A big, northern kind of baby with watery blue eyes. I have suddenly become quite busy, feeding and taking care of the baby. I don't at all have the physical sense of having borne a baby, but I believe that this signifies a reproduction and continuation of consciousness, which I take to be a good sign. It seems to be the child of Klaus Dose, but if this is the child of the Klaus who struggled in life and died young, I worry about the future of this child. I slightly graze my head.

Letters

There are numerous envelopes neatly lined up on the desk and they all seem to be letters for K. On the envelope are exaggerated rose patterns that are raised, like wallpaper, and K is looking at the desk and taking the letters.

Port of Bizerte

I arrive by ship at the port of Bizerte in Tunisia. Though it is day, the place is washed in the colors of dusk and it feels like I have never seen the place before, even though I have. I begin to walk, finding green apples growing in someone's yard, when suddenly there is a man looming nearby who calls out to me, saying he'll give me apples. I was fine just looking, but I carelessly go into the yard.

Some kind of a large tray is affixed inside the pond, where a few waterfowl are floating. There are some cracks in the dried dirt upon this tray that is separated from the water in the pond. I gaze upon it, puzzled, when the man says, "This way the birds naturally become taxidermically stuffed specimens," as if this was the most appropriate way to handle them. And then he says to himself, "This is the first time that a journalist has come," and invites me into a farmhouse-like home. The ceiling and tatami room are rigged: he tugs at a pull ring to reveal the numerous mannequins with elaborate Japanese costumes stored inside.

Although I hadn't even planned my itinerary, the man says, "Your ship leaves at four o'clock," and restlessly hurries me back to the port. I do as he says, letting him accompany me to the ticket booth at the port. I leave my black bag with him and go to the restroom, but when I return he is not there.

By the time the ship leaves, night has closed in completely upon the jetty I now run along. I witness the man throwing my black bag into the ocean. "There are poems in there," I shout, but it is too late. In my black bag, my only piece of luggage, is some money and a folder containing my entire poetry manuscript. The poems are ruined; the bag sinks into the dark ocean. Then the man takes his seat as the port watchman at this jetty, closes the latch on a steel, single-person, ticket gate-like enclosure, and is completely insolent, ignoring all.

S's body

The lady stares at S's body and says, "You are thin." On S's body is a transparent kind of fabric, or it is covered by the flow of water—it bears a faint, finely refracted shadow. I wonder from where I am watching this scene.

Crutches

"I always told *you* everything," I say in a hushed voice, asking Y about the person he is currently seeing, though he is unwilling to reveal anything. He never told me about Lino either, until it was completely over. I feel a crushing feeling in my heart, in which I just can't ascertain anything at all. I suddenly notice that Y is standing in the faint darkness outside with a crutch under each arm. A light shines only on the part where the crutches are, distinctly as if through a pattern. I think—Oh, so that's what it was—and feel that I shouldn't have pressed him that way about it.

Beauty, that

Someone is showing me a picture made on drawing paper. It seems to be of a publisher's building; the steps to the entrance are drawn in a convoluted kind of way. Casually I look sideways at the picture and see an image of a human. Several other drawings show a human when you change the orientation, but they are all rather flat. Even as I change the orientation of the drawing, a tightly knit texture should be wafting over the whole. That, I think, is beauty.

R u n n i n g   p o s t u r e

I am being chased and so I run, though the problem lies not in the fact that someone is chasing me, but in the posture with which I run away.

Pool without water

There is no water in the pool. Nevertheless, I decide to try to swim by putting up the lane ropes and assuming that there is water. I feel around behind me but I cannot find the rope. I think that if only I could find it I would be able to swim.

As a small snake

As we walk side by side, I reach my arm around behind, where it turns into a vine or a small snake and entangles with the arm, so that we are holding hands behind us. After walking only a few steps, I can feel the backside of the person's chest, and am unusually calm. It is a strapping person.

Heavy heart

That night when I enter with a heavy heart the church that looks like a ruin, there is talk of living and working at the Chinese restaurant in the back. This might solve my housing problem, but I doubt anything will come of it. I am inclined to think that it would be impossible for me to work every day.

I leave my bags at the Chinese restaurant and go to Y's apartment, even though it is late. Y has already lost his youthfulness sleeping there with stubble on his face. He suddenly awakens; he seems like a different person as he kisses me and tries to pull me into bed. Japanese children's kimonos are sloppily piled up in a corner of the room, and when I ask what happened here, he says there was a big sale so he bought them. I find it strange that there would be a sale on Japanese kimonos in a foreign country. In bed Y wears something like a sleeveless brown ballet practice outfit. A serum drips from his side; several blood vessels hang down too. When he catches me looking, he says, "This is my spinal fluid," as if it were nothing, and lifts a blood vessel as if lifting a piece of thread. I can't take it any more and go to leave. Y gets up and accompanies me to the station.

I manage to get on the last train of the night and ride it to town, and now have to find a hotel.

At the site

In a mountain studio, the bed that I had shared with K. It is still too sad for me to sleep. K's wife and several men in uniform arrive to investigate. She is an intellectual type and I don't feel any reproach from her; she simply calmly verifies the site. K must have run off to some remote location, as he is nowhere to be seen. She is completely understanding of this as well—something in her gaze upon me feels like how one would look upon a victim. They seem to have another site to investigate, so the group wraps it up and takes off in a hurry. After that I am left behind in that desolate room.

Paper with scattered dreams

I have both a pet dog and a pet squirrel and I worry about what to feed the squirrel; in the pale blue moments before dawn I try to tag along with my dad on his walk while chanting a sutra; I can see numerous red ants; I am holding money I earned from interpreting; and I have a small box that dispenses stamps when you press a button. I now casually try to fold up and place in my pocket this paper, scattered with such fragments of dreams.

Old actress

The old actress is threatened by impending peril, so we decide to trade hotel rooms and keys. When I enter the room I see that it has mirror-covered walls with prominent use of marble—it is a grand but intimidating room. Beyond that I see a small room in the back where several young men sleep on the floor in their sleeping bags. I prod the half-sleeping young men to come outside, denouncing, "Look, here is the source of your peril," from a platform covered in white cloth. They are outfitted for a trip with a modern Japanese youth group.

Poetry collection

In my new collection of poetry, there is water moistening the open page—and numerous, very small babies are trapped inside as if they have been drawn there.

Unknown land

The ship drifts ashore on the wharf of an unknown land. Among the passengers is a man headed for London, carrying a large suitcase and panicking. I myself disembark, thinking that it's perfectly fine to have arrived at an unknown land. There are few people in this city; an Asian sort of loneliness wafts in the air. I wonder where this is and what language people speak. Wanting to buy a newspaper, I look for a kiosk on the street. None of the kiosks have anything but a few sundries, and no newspapers. Thinking I might learn something about the city, I enter a church. Inside it's a little like a Buddhist temple; I see some young Japanese people there, so it turns out that there are Japanese people living in such a place. Eventually I learn that this is Jamaica—and if this is Jamaica, then it must be the Jamaican language they speak—and I feel slightly invigorated.

Death by shooting

It appears that only one of us will be shot to death, so they make us form two lines outside. Because of the way we are positioned I figure out that that person is me. There are young children in the lines too. I beg them to send everyone away because the sound of the shooting will linger in the children's memories and be traumatic, so then I am left alone with the officer. When I die, I should no longer be able to think. I am holding my breath. For some reason the officer disappears. And then my younger sister says in a calm voice, "Let's trade places." My sister runs away through the shadowy fields in order to trick the other officer who is coming this way, and the officer chases after her.

Two pieces of cloth

"Knead and mix them together," I am instructed—so I try to do so, but when I take a closer look they are two thin pieces of cloth and it is very difficult to get them to mix together.

Flute

I have a flute in my hands and try to play it, but no sound comes
out. I accidentally breathe in and something like a scrap of silver
foil gets left behind in my mouth. As I am wondering what it's
like inside the flute, the thin wooden flute splits vertically like a
cicada shell, exposing the metallic scraps and grass seed mixed
inside. The flute sounds because of something inside it. I put it
back together and try again to play it. Still no sound comes out.

Afterword: On Ayane Kawata

Ayane Kawata does not mingle in Tokyo with the other Japanese poets. She does not give readings, attend conferences, participate in *taidan* (formal conversations that are recorded and later transcribed and published), write reviews, or judge contests—her physical presence is almost invisible in the poetic communities of Japan—but throughout the years her work has continued to be published by many of the most prominent poetry journals and publishers in Japan. Her work is not part of any movement, group, or *dojinshi* (a coterie journal), and she is not associated with any of the *joseishi* (women's poetry) movements of postwar Japanese poetry. If Kawata identifies herself as a poet, she does so simply because she writes poems, and not because of any tangible stature or public recognition as a famous poet. Poetry is not a career for her, though poetry is her way of living.

And if poetry is not a career, then, Kawata also sees little need for her work to be translated into other languages. It is only with the encouragement of Takashi Hiraide, the enthusiasm of American readers, and the strong support from E. Tracy Grinnell at Litmus Press that this book has come to exist at all, and that we were able to receive Kawata's permission to publish this book. Even as her translator, I have had almost no direct contact with Kawata herself, and thus, although the poet is living, any mistakes in this translation are entirely my responsibility.

I first encountered Ayane Kawata's work through her Gendaishi Bunko. The Gendaishi Bunko is a paperback series of selected or collected poems by major Japanese poets, published by Shichosha, the monolithic publishing force behind much of contemporary Japanese poetry. Since the 1960s, the series has published close to 200 of these volumes, of which Kawata's was #122. Her volume was published in 1994 and collects six books in total, from her first book, *Time of Sky* (Kumo Publishers, 1969), through her second to last complete book at the time, *Castles in the Air — A dream journal* (Shoshi Yamada, 1991).

::::::::::::::::

Kawata is considered a Japanese poet only because she writes in Japanese—she has not lived in Japan for most of her life. She was not even born in Japan—she was born in 1940 in the city of Qiqihar in the Heilongjiang Province of northeast China during the Japanese occupation of the region. She lived with her family in Manchuria until the age of 5, at which point they returned to Japan, to live at first in Saitama prefecture, then the city of Kobe.

After abandoning earlier attempts to pursue a life of music or visual art, she married an atomic physicist and moved to

Hokkaido—it was only then that Kawata began reading in earnest. About seven years later, in 1969, she produced her first poetry collection, *Time of Sky*. At the time it was published, Kawata had no personal connections to any poets and simply mailed a copy of the book to poets and artists she admired. She quickly made a strong impression on the literary community, garnering praise from such luminaries as Taruho Inagaki, Tatsuhiko Shibusawa, and Koichi Iijima. They wrote her letters, sent her artwork, and invited her to visit.

At this point, Kawata was well positioned and on track to become a major poet in Japan, and as proof, she received solicitations to submit poems to major publications. Often a Japanese poet is invited to write a series of poems for the same publication, regularly and under deadline. Kawata gave this a try, and published a few poems in the well-known poetry magazine *Eureka*. She quickly decided that this mode of writing was not for her, however. The poems she wrote at this time were an attempt to further develop the ideas in *Time of Sky*, and although she chose to never collect these poems in book form, they are the ones that first caught Takashi Hiraide's attention. Of them, he says,

> Each of them was made of a chain of images that were extremely purified. But sustained therewithin was something that necessitated serious regard—a kind of tension that had sucked in a vast amount of the atmosphere, as

well as a stirring towards metamorphosis that surrenders the self to undulations coming out of nowhere.

Uninterested in following the conventional path to becoming a poet in Japan, and perhaps also with the desire to escape, Kawata soon left the country to take an art-study tour of Italy, where she has since chosen to live most of her life. In addition to living in various parts of Italy, she also spent varying amounts of time living in France, Switzerland, and London.

After her move to Italy, her work changed radically in a number of ways, moving away from the abstract, surreal imagery and the terse, incongruous syntactic constructions found in *Time of Sky*, to a more narrative verse that depicts characters and landscape set in Italy and Europe. These works are collected in the books *Pisa Dori* (Pisa Avenue), *Himei* (Scream), and *Asa no kafe* (Morning Café), as well as *Sākasu no yoru* (Circus Night), which is a collection of prose poetry. More recently, several of Kawata's books, including *Unnan* (Yunnan) (Shichosha, 2003) and *Deido* (Mud) (Arisusha, 2000) have been based on her travels to China, the country of her birth.

When Kawata wrote *Time of Sky*, she claims to have felt that she was only capable of writing very short poems. She proved herself wrong, however, as most of her poetry since then has been in the form of longer, lyric verse. Her sixth publication, *Castles in the Air*, is also something of a divergence from the bulk of her oeuvre and has a completely different method of composition from her other work. Its poems are derived from a notebook the author kept for 15 years, in which she recorded her dreams every morning upon waking. From there she selected and edited the pieces that were collected in the book. The logic in these prose poems may feel familiar to us as dream logic, but we also find in them the complexity and anxiety attendant to a lifetime spent living in a culture not one's own, an ongoing reckoning with one's dangers and desires, and the difficulty (and absurdity) of trying to communicate with others. Kawata also notes in an interview that at the moment she completed this book, she ceased to remember any dreams at all.

::::::::::::::::

As often espoused in the "nomad poetics" of Pierre Joris, the state of being estranged or displaced can be seen as the very site of poetry. Kawata, too, describes much of her life in a nomadic fashion, and sees the act of living and the act of writing both as continuous searches, always in flux and never arriving nor resolving. It is the border space that Lyn Hejinian writes of:

> The border is not an edge along the fringe of society and experience but rather their very middle—their between; it names the condition of doubt and encounter which

being foreign to a situation (which may be life itself) provokes—

[Lyn Hejinian, *Language of Inquiry*]

In Kawata's case, both the action and the location fold into each other:

Traveling the endless noonday street in the eyes of myself traveling the endless noonday street in my eyes

[#39, *Time of Sky*]

Hejinian's border space is one of incongruities and dispossession, an unstable site where one might "see larks in a sky without larks." Or the body is served by its vocal proxy: "Screams are forced to run radiantly and full speed." Of these small packages of surreal logic in *Time of Sky*, the modernist scholar and critic Kaichi Nakano said:

[Her poems] exhibit crystalline—or perhaps elementary— sparks, but what's interesting is that they are not so much of sensations or images, but instead they manifest their function in a beautiful world of the Idea.

[Kaichi Nakano, insert for *Time of Sky*]

Kawata's universe is also one where the intensity of life itself is precarious, oblique, and threatening:

I hold a cup, trying to drink the blood coursing through it, but I just can't bring myself to drink it.

[Cup of blood, *Castles in the Air*]

The diamonds tear the sky apart and convulse the blood by daybreak to the very last drop

[#90, *Time of Sky*]

When asked in an interview about the images of death in her work and at what times they occur to her, Kawata replied: "Every day. I always think this could be the last day. That tension always exists with me."

Sawako Nakayasu
Tokyo, February 2010

::::::::::::::

All unattributed quotes are from the Gendaishi Bunko, including quotes from Kawata that are taken from an interview.

::::::::::::::

I wish to thank the editors of the following publications, in which some of the translations have been previously published, sometimes in earlier versions: *Aufgabe, Mantis, Octopus,* and the

2010 PEN Translation Feature. Excerpts of this translation may also be found in *Factorial,* edited by myself.

A very special thanks goes out to Joshua Edwards and Eugene Kang for reading earlier drafts of the manuscript, and E. Tracy Grinnell for all her support in making this book happen.

Sawako Nakayasu

Sawako Nakayasu was born in Japan and has lived mostly in the US since the age of six. Her books include *Texture Notes* (Letter Machine Editions, 2010), *Hurry Home Honey* (Burning Deck, 2009), *Nothing fictional but the accuracy or arrangement (she,* (Quale Press, 2005), and *So we have been given time Or,* (Verse Press, 2004). Books of translations include *For the Fighting Spirit of the Walnut* by Takashi Hiraide (New Directions, 2008) which won the 2009 Best Translated Book Award from Three Percent, as well as *Four From Japan* (Litmus Press / Belladonna Books, 2006) featuring four contemporary poets, and *To the Vast Blooming Sky* (Seeing Eye Books), a chapbook of poems by the Japanese modernist Chika Sagawa. Nakayasu has received fellowships from the NEA and PEN, and her own work has been translated into Japanese, Swedish, Arabic, Chinese, and Vietnamese.

Litmus Press Titles

Portrait of Colon Dash Parenthesis, Jeffrey Jullich, $15
Hyperglossia, Stacy Szymaszek, $15
From Dame Quickly, Jennifer Scappettone, $15
Face Before Against, Isabelle Garron, $15
    translated by Sarah Riggs
Animate, Inanimate Aims, Brenda Iijima $15
Fruitlands, Kate Colby, $12
Counter Daemons, Roberto Harrison, $15
Emptied of All Ships, Stacy Szymaszek, $12
Inner China, Eva Sjödin, $12
    translated by Jennifer Hayashida
The Mudra, Kerri Sonnenberg, $12
Another Kind of Tenderness, Xue Di, $15
    translated by Keith Waldrop, Forrest Gander, Stephen Thomas,
    Theodore Deppe, and Sue Ellen Thompson
Euclid Shudders, Mark Tardi, $12
Notebooks: 1956–1978, Danielle Collobert, $12
    translated by Norma Cole
The House Seen from Nowhere, Keith Waldrop, $12

Published in collaboration with Belladonna Books:

NO GENDER: Reflections on the Life & Work of kari edwards
    edited by Julian T. Brolaski, erica kaufman, and E. Tracy Grinnell, $18
Bharat jiva, kari edwards, $15
Four From Japan: Contemporary Poetry & Essays by Women
    translated and with an introduction by Sawako Nakayasu, $14

www.litmuspress.org

green press
INITIATIVE

Litmus Press is committed to preserving ancient forests and natural resources. We elected to print this title on 30% post consumer recycled paper, processed chlorine free. As a result, for this printing, we have saved:

2 Trees (40' tall and 6-8" diameter)
1,070 Gallons of Wastewater
1 million BTU's of Total Energy
65 Pounds of Solid Waste
222 Pounds of Greenhouse Gases

Litmus Press made this paper choice because our printer, Thomson-Shore, Inc., is a member of Green Press Initiative, a nonprofit program dedicated to supporting authors, publishers, and suppliers in their efforts to reduce their use of fiber obtained from endangered forests.
For more information, visit www.greenpressinitiative.org.

Environmental impact estimates were made using the Environmental Defense Paper Calculator. For more information visit: www.papercalculator.org.